Getting Noticed on Twitter in 2C
Start Guide, Sonic L
First Ed

Published by Sonic UX
London, United Kingdom.

Table of Contents

Chapter 1: Introduction   *3*

Chapter 2: Building a Following   *6*

Chapter 3: Creating Engaging Content   *11*

Chapter 4: Understanding Trends   *15*

Chapter 5: Getting Verified   *19*

Chapter 6: Twitter Follower Ratio   *23*

Chapter 7: Your Bio   *25*

Chapter 8: What is SEO and Why Does it Matter?   *28*

Chapter 9: Influencers   *33*

Chapter 10: Twitter Analytics   *35*

Chapter 11: Making the Most of Twitter   *39*

Chapter 1: Introduction

Wasim Ahmed and Marc Bonne

There was once a world without social media platforms where brands would rely on traditional marketing techniques such as having a visible high-street presence, newspaper advertisements and leaflets. Then, the advent of the Internet and the World Wide Web, gave rise to online marketing. Brands now draw upon various online platforms in order to increase brand visibility and capture new customers.

Since its inception in March 2006 (Weller *et al.*, 2014), Twitter has brought people together to engage in conversation, in real time. Alongside the rise of specific types of social media platforms in the early years of the 21st century such as MySpace, Bebo and Facebook, Twitter offered something unique due to its open and public nature. On Twitter, anyone can follow anyone, and it provides brands with a channel to communicate with customers.

Twitter provides the ability for users to send 280-character text updates known as 'tweets', which were originally limited to 140 characters from 2006 to September 2017 (Telegraph, 2017). Users of Twitter have grown over the years and now over 320 million people have an active account (Twitter Q1 2017 Company Metrics, 2017). It has been a major part of world events (Downing and Dron, 2019), whilst being a source of news with Twitter often making headlines itself through viral hashtags (Downing and Ahmed, 2019).

Brands have always sought exposure to potential customers and Twitter provides the ability for organic and paid exposure to massive audiences. Brands should take Twitter seriously, as those who get it right can see their profits increase and improve brand image.

We decided to write this book in order to guide anyone looking to gain traction on Twitter. This book will teach you how to navigate Twitter, get noticed and ultimately build a loyal following. We will go through all the tools and features available that you might never have heard of. We will also cover the basics of creating engaging content that stops the user mid scroll.

We're both passionate about social media and have worked with some large scale organizations on social media projects and online marketing-related products. We're also both academics and enjoy teaching and researching social media.

We hope that by the final chapter, you'll understand how to implement campaigns, review your results in Twitter analytics and target users who are most likely to engage with you, your products and services. We'll also touch on some more advance methods of analyzing Twitter data and identifying influential users.

References

Downing, J., & Dron, R. (2019). Tweeting Grenfell: Discourse and networks in critical constructions of British Muslim social boundaries on social media. *new media & society*, 1461444819864572.

Downing, J., & Ahmed, W. (2019). # MacronLeaks as a "warning shot" for European democracies: challenges to election blackouts presented by social media and election meddling during the 2017 French presidential election. *French Politics*, 1-22.

Twitter Q1 2017 Company Metrics. (2017). Number of monthly active Twitter users worldwide from 1st quarter 2010 to 1st quarter 2017 (in millions). *Statista*. Retrieved 19 June, 2017, from https://www.statista.com/statistics/282087/number-of-monthly-active-twitter-users/.

Telegraph (2017, November 7). Twitter is letting everyone post 280 character tweets. The Telegraph. Retrieved from http://www.telegraph.co.uk/technology/2017/11/07/twitter-letting-everyone-post-280-character-tweets/

Weller, K., Bruns, A., Burgess, J. E., Merja, M.,& Puschmann, C. (2014). Twitter and society: An introduction. In: K. Weller, A. Bruns, J. Burgess, M. Mahrt & C. Puschmann (Eds.), Twitter and Society. New York: Peter Lang, New York.

Chapter 2: Building a Following

Marc Bonne and Wasim Ahmed

One of the most important aspects of social media is having a good following of users who engage with your content. It is crucial to place yourself or business in a particular market, ensuring that your posts are seen by the most relevant users to your product and/or service. Finding and identifying a niche to focus on is really important as it, in turn, defines an audience.

It is important to not fall into the trap of thinking most people will like you or your product; whilst you might have the aspirations of Coca-Cola, you probably don't have the marketing budget or brand recognition to compete with them in the same way.

Moreover, a generic profile, content and branding will ensure you fade out in the never ending scroll of posts. So it is important to make sure that you have a catchy, profile with good branding. This will make it more likely that a user would follow you.We can look at an example of the Twitter account of the University of Sheffield provided in figure 2.1 below.

Figure 2.1 University of Sheffield's Twitter account

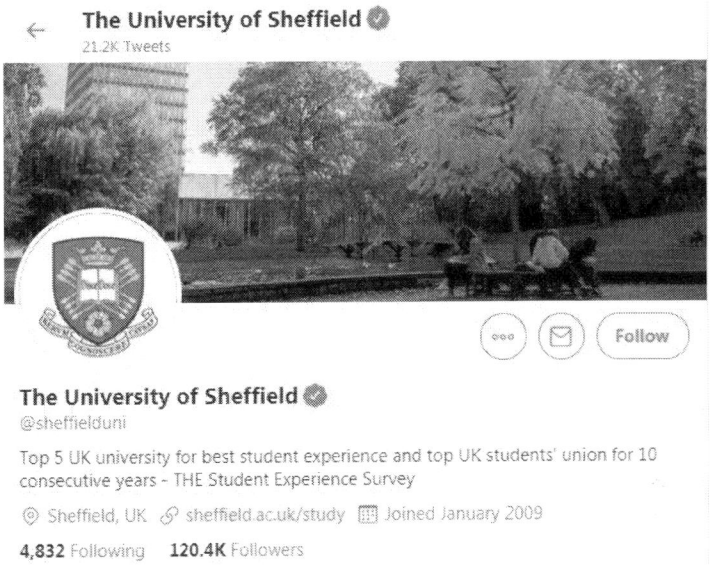

The University of Sheffield ✓
21.2K Tweets

The University of Sheffield ✓
@sheffielduni

Top 5 UK university for best student experience and top UK students' union for 10 consecutive years - THE Student Experience Survey

◎ Sheffield, UK 🔗 sheffield.ac.uk/study 📅 Joined January 2009

4,832 Following   **120.4K** Followers

The Twitter account has a brand-based profile picture, a powerful bio and a relevant website to pick up potential leads. We will look more at the Twitter bio in Chapter 7. The banner features autumn scenery at a park near the University. You should design and develop your own brand-based profile based on key touchpoints with your customers. It is important to have the profile checked by potential customers and colleagues for feedback and refinement. Avoid the mistake of adding poor quality images as your profile and/or banner picture. You would be surprised by the number of brands with poor quality images!

Once you have a suitable profile, you have to find your audience. Therefore, your Twitter profile should immediately start following other Twitter users including large and small accounts, but most importantly, these must be relevant accounts so your posts are seen and retweeted by those who will be interested in your product/service. A key aspect is to produce and share content that is going to generate value to your Twitter followers.

For instance, if you are a cake shop, you may wish to share easy to make cake recipes on Twitter and/or produce content on your website or blog that you can share on Twitter. By providing value, you will naturally receive followers and Twitter users who are keen to engage with your brand.

If you sell cars, you may wish to follow users who are at an age where they've recently passed their test. You can also examine who your average customer may be, their age, gender, income level and highest education. Targeting which accounts you're following from the very beginning will equal more engagement in the future.

In terms of where to look first for other accounts to follow, it is best to target those that are relevant using the standard search function, but also utilize your existing social media accounts and email contacts. We're also going to introduce some tools you can use later in this chapter. LinkedIn, in particular, is a good site to migrate contacts from, especially if your business targets other businesses for your product or services i.e. not public-facing.
You are more likely to be followed by someone you already have a relationship with. It is quite easy to

migrate your contacts from LinkedIn to Twitter; visit your LinkedIn contacts page then choose "settings." You'll have the option to export your contacts into a .CSV file. The file can then be seamlessly uploaded to your email account. Then from Twitter, you should be able to import your email contacts.

There are other methods to find relevant Twitter accounts; services like Tweepi (https://tweepi.com/) allow you to see a list of accounts that follow your own followers on Twitter and then target those users. Many of these services like Tweepi are available for free. Also, it is possible to follow accounts recommended by Twitter; these accounts are usually the followers of followers who share similar interests and have similar demographics. These accounts can also be worth following.

You may also have an established following on Instagram, Facebook, SnapChat or WhatsApp. You should cross-promote to gain even more followers on these platforms. This can be as simple as alerting your followers and contacts on these platforms to follow you on Twitter by providing them with your user-handle. You could also incentivize this process by offering the first 10,000 followers a discount voucher and/or chance for a price.

The online tool, Audiense (https://audiense.com/), which has a limited free and paid account, provides a great ability to significantly increase your following in your relevant area. It enables users to search all of Twitter using various specialized filters, which massively goes beyond   the   standard   Twitter   Search.

For instance, Audiense can be utilized to identify all Twitter users in Sheffield, UK that have an interest in Data Science. If an organization was planning an event related to Data Science, then this information would be gold, as it could alert the individuals about the event. We are aware of organizations and individuals making thousands of pounds by using some of these methods.

It is also possible to search your own Twitter followers for personalized marketing possibilities. Audiense is packed with other features such as the ability to determine the best time to tweet everyday (based on when your followers are most active). This is a great feature because if you are tweeting when your most influential followers are not active, then you have a smaller chance of your messages being seen.

Chapter 3: Creating Engaging Content

Wasim Ahmed and Marc Bonne

To attract an audience and even just place your Twitter account so that relevant accounts follow, retweet you and ultimately grow your business, you have to consistently create engaging content. Many businesses fail to do this, presuming the users will be just as interested in their services or products as they are.

Keeping your content fresh and relevant to current affairs and developments in your industry, is one way to "piggyback" on subjects that others are already discussing. To do this, you need to be following these events as they happen. Notifications from services like Google Alerts (https://www.google.co.uk/alerts) and checking through trending hashtags on Twitter can help you respond creatively in a way that is targeted and in real-time. In figure 3.1 below, we can see a great example of this from Disney Music.

Figure 3.1 – Disney Music's Tweet on Mother's Day

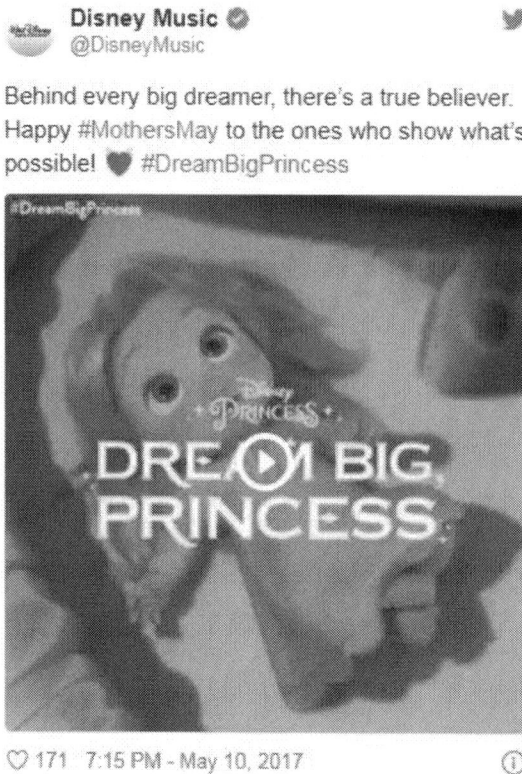

Disney Music ✓
@DisneyMusic

Behind every big dreamer, there's a true believer.
Happy #MothersMay to the ones who show what's
possible! ♥ #DreamBigPrincess

♡ 171   7:15 PM - May 10, 2017   ⓘ

In the example above, Disney Music piggy backs on the trending hashtag at the time, which was Mother's day, where users were using the hashtag '#MothersMay'.

Furthermore, having relevant posts that hit your target market is the 'quality' aspect, engaging whoever may be reading it. Unlike in other social media platforms, Twitter does not prescribe to the quality over quantity principle; on Twitter, it is fine to repeat tweets several times across the day. It is also important to remember and keep in mind different time-zones. The more you tweet, the more followers you're likely to gain and retain.

When you are generating a large volume of tweets, you can also test tweets, images, the tone and overall voice of your Twitter account to see which types of tweets receive more engagement.

It is an iterative process and it is always important to review what you tweet, the subjects along with the type of media that can engage your audience; thus, you can adjust your tweeting accordingly. Be mindful of who your audience is during this process; it is less useful if your tweets are getting a high volume of retweets and feedback from an audience that is uninterested in your product and/or service.

The end goal, of course, is to convert this traffic into sales and when done effectively, it can bring in additional customers. Twitter followers are more likely to buy a product or service if they are already following you.

It is best to think of tweeting as a constant trickle; whilst the individual tweet may not take up much time, think of it as a side task you do throughout the day, when on public transport, at the gym or waiting for a train.

Producing highly relevant content alongside a high volume of tweets where you constantly react to content online is time-consuming. So it is often good practice to schedule your tweets using sites like Hootsuite (https://hootsuite.com/en-gb/) so you can keep your tweeting going throughout the day. Hootsuite and other similar tools are utilized by most brands to automate content delivery. A brand may schedule tweets for an entire month in only a couple of days. Hootsuite will then automatically send out the tweets. Using such tools can save you a lot of time.

Another good tip to use (if it is appropriate to your audience) is to use inspirational quotes. In the endless scroll, a quick quote in a large font can often cut through; these are also low maintenance and easy to generate either by a search engine or apps.

Memes either retweeted or created by yourself can be a way of reaching audiences and images and videos are integral to your tweets; however, try to add a link to your website that makes sense to the meme. Memes, images and videos are an opportunity for a business to really express itself creatively and stand apart from the crowd.

Be aware that they are difficult to get right and with existing memes, there is a shelf-life beyond which your site can become dated if you continue to tweet them.

The exact time of sharing a tweet e.g., morning, afternoon, or evening may affect how many impressions and engagements it will gain, so don't be afraid of sharing similar content throughout the day. This is especially true if you have an international following. Table 3.1, below, adapted from Kawasaki and Fitzpatrick (2014) highlights that it is fine to send similar messages across the day on Twitter as compared to other platforms.

Table 3.1 Comparison of Tweeting Volumes across Platforms per Day

PLATFORM	CASUAL USERS	INTENSE USERS
FACEBOOK	1-2	3-4
LINKEDIN	1	4
TWITTER	8-12	25

References

Kawasaki, G., & Fitzpatrick, P. (2014). *The art of social media: Power tips for power users*. Penguin.

Chapter 4: Understanding Trends
Marc Bonne and Wasim Ahmed

Having touched on Twitter trends in the previous chapter, we will explore trends more deeply in this chapter. Jumping on to Twitter trends i.e., a 'trending topic' allows your tweet to be seen by those who are also interested in the same trend and can be used as an opportunity to engage other users and comment on their tweets, ballooning the trend as a whole and your business alongside that. When a business uses a trending hashtag in a post, you expose that message to everyone discussing that topic and looking at the tweets relevant to that.

First, you need to know where to find such trends. Twitter is where people connect with their interests and passions; tapping into that may be difficult, but you can use events on a local scale, for example, a programmer convention in your local area. Many businesses struggle with essentially talking to individuals as a business and making that conversation feel authentic.

Very general tweets on a popular hashtag can look as though you're inserting yourself into a conversation without having anything to say, just for the sake of it. You'll add value if you're specific and add some personality to your business. Adapt your tweets on a timely hashtag and pivot back to your product or service.

A conversation that may not directly relate to your product/service may still resonate with your company's values; for example, a climate activist trend and a business that has recycling at its heart. These can often be a more relatable and easier conversation to have with other users than pivoting back to your product; don't be shy, a heartfelt approach is often most effective. Figure 4.1 below is an example of piggybacking on a trending topic from the Salvation Army.

Figure 4.1 – Piggybacking on a Trend

At the time, the hashtag '#whiteandgold' was trending, which was a viral internet sensation where online users debated the color of a dress. The Salvation Army Piggy backed on the trend to raise awareness of domestic abuse against women. If you're generally new to Twitter, then there are some pitfalls that businesses and personal users fall into that are best to avoid.

- Avoid over tagging. There should really be only one or two hashtags in any one post as a general rule. Spam tagging is not advised; for example, "#topgun #flight #simulations for #throwbackthursdays"; while on other platforms (Instagram), this is the norm these can be seen as opportunistic and inauthentic on Twitter. Good topics to tag can be events, annual holidays or celebrations; popular media such as music videos or a TV series, days of the week and general interest topics.
- Be sensitive to the events you're reacting to. Serious incidents should be treated as such and an insensitive tweet around national emergency could have serious backlash.
- If you're launching a hashtag for an original campaign, complete a hashtag search before you begin to ensure it isn't already being used by someone who would eclipse your message.
- Keep hashtags relatively short, preferably less than three words.

Creating your own hashtags can be useful when launching a new campaign or promotion; they can even be a slogan tied to your brand, such as Nike's #justdoit marketing campaign, which are constantly being pushed, or specific campaigns on a new product line or season. Getting those already purchasing your product or service to tweet reviews using your hashtag perhaps in exchange for a discount on their next order can be a useful way of spreading the online word-of-mouth to your customer's friends, family and followers. A review from a friend on Twitter is generally more powerful than from someone you don't know. Below is a list of useful websites to help you find Twitter trends:

- Twitter (https://twitter.com/). Clearly has the most up to date and reliable data.
- Trendsmap (https://www.trendsmap.com/). Look up trending hashtags via location.
- Sprout Social. Trends (https://sproutsocial.com/). Report analyzes all of your incoming messages and shows which hashtags are trending with your personal brand.
- RiteTag (https://ritetag.com/). Gives a list of trending hashtags, as well as feedback on your hashtags as you type, which indicates the strength of your Twitter hashtag.
- #tagdef (https://tagdef.com/en/) lists popular hashtags by time frame, including current, weekly and all time most popular hashtags. Tagdef is also great since the site provides a short description for each hashtag, making it easier for your business to sift through the topic before jumping in.
- Hashtagify (https://hashtagify.me/) can tell you which hashtags are correlated and used alongside other hashtags.
- Tagboard (https://tagboard.readme.io/docs/getting-started-with-tagboard-its-as-easy-as-1-2-3) allows you to see the comments associated with any given hashtag

Chapter 5: Getting Verified

Wasim Ahmed and Marc Bonne

Up until recently, verified status on Twitter was something easy to come by as Twitter launched an online form for anyone to complete. However, they have now shut this system down.

One of the downsides of Twitter is that they've still not managed to fix their verification system. The current system seems unfair for smaller brands and individuals, as it is opaque and certain users will be verified even without an operating verification system.

A verification tick on Twitter is hugely beneficial for those viewing you to believe you are an authentic thriving business; often, without it, you can't be taken seriously by your competitors or customers so it is important to achieve verification. So it is a real shame that Twitter has not put 'fixing their verification system' on their priority list.

However, Twitter verification could be reactivated at any time. So it is to put as much authentic information into your profile as possible and then fill out the verification form provided by Twitter once it is reactivated in the future. It is important to make sure that you:

- Fill out your profile fully with profile picture, cover photo, name, website and detailed bio.

- Add a verified phone number and confirm your email address.
- Add your birthday.
- Set your tweets as "public".
- Visit the verification form on Twitter.

One of the biggest factors for verification on Twitter is that the profile is of "public interest", which can be a confusingly vague term for businesses to aim for. It is a subjective process and is not always clear.

To provide some clarity on what is meant by "public interest", Twitter lists public figures and organizations in the world of Music, TV, Film, Fashion, Government, Politics, Religion, Journalism, Media, Sports and Business. If you are a legitimate business that is known in your field or in your location, it should be enough for you to be considered.

There are a couple of methods you can utilize to make your business look legitimate:

- A consistently active profile over a few weeks.
- Link to other verified Twitter accounts in your bio, for example; a supplier, industry body employers and past employers.
- Be as specific as you can about the location of your business.
- On the verification form, you are asked to submit a minimum of 2 links; try to submit the maximum number of links.
- You can also see other accounts that have been recently verified by visiting the Twitter account

@verfied and comparing them to your own account to see what's missing.

You could be asked for more information to show that your business is something that people are interested in or know about.

The process is about proving to be trustworthy; if you can demonstrate that, you should be in with a chance. If not, build up the business review the tips listed above and try again at a later date.

Chapter 6: Twitter Follower Ratio

Marc Bonne and Wasim Ahmed

The ratio of your Twitter followers to the Twitter accounts you follow can be a difficult thing to manage and while it is advised that you follow accounts that are relevant to your business, it is important not to over follow.

If you follow a significantly higher number of people than follow you, it can send a message to those viewing your account that you're inauthentic or amateurish. When you are beginning the process of building up your Twitter following, it may be unavoidable.

Usually referred to as the golden ratio, it is an indicator of your success on Twitter. Twitter accounts of celebrities and well-known entities like Tesla or Elton John will have "positive ratios", meaning they have more followers than those they're following.

In the extreme, it can be the case that Twitter users viewing your profile may doubt that you're a human/ business, as there is a large problem of bots on Twitter who are created either to cause mischief online or can be bought by less reputable companies to boost their own following. For example, if an account follows 360,000, it is most likely that the account is a bot account mass following indiscriminately; being confused with a bot is a bad look for business, when that first impression looking at your profile will take seconds and the user will simply move on.

Of course, the inverse is true, but much more difficult to achieve. When an account is following a relatively small number of accounts with a large following itself, it sends the message that you or your company clearly has something to say that others are interested in and is more likely to gain followers. So you may want to develop either a 1:1 follower or follower ratio or follow slightly less users than who follow your account.

Chapter 7: Your Bio

Wasim Ahmed and Marc Bonne

Your Twitter bio is the second point of engagement on Twitter, with the tweet that leads the user there being the first. You should aim to achieve two things with your bio originality and impact. Think of the millions of Twitter bios; ask yourself the question, *'which Twitter bio do I remember?'* The answer is probably none.

Being original is not as easy as it oftentimes sounds; we think we're being original, however, our bios are just a subconscious mashup of terrible bios read in the past. We can take a look at the Twitter bio of Wendy's, a fast food outlet, in figure of 7.1.

Figure 7.1 Wendy's Twitter Bio

Wendy's ✓
@Wendys

We like our tweets the same way we like to make our hamburgers: better than anyone expects from a fast food joint.

⌕ feastoflegends.com 🗓 Joined July 2009

444 Following **3.4M** Followers

Many fall into the trap of over hash-tagging; whilst it may be a logical step, as hashtags are easy to find and a fundamental part of Twitter's algorithms, the vast majority of accounts with more than a million followers use no hashtags at all in their bio. This is because excessive hash-tagging is bad Twitter etiquette! It is seen as spam, contrived and part of a transparent strategy, which is everything you want to avoid. Over hash-tagging is prejudicial to gaining followers; in short, it puts users off.

Furthermore, Twitter bios have a character limit of 160, meaning you are using space that could otherwise be utilized to convey your brand ethos, images and values. On Twitter, character count is absolutely crucial and while shorter tweets may be appropriate, the characters in your bio are your first impression, so a detailed, creative and original bio, can help you and your business stand out.

Examine your successful competitors for how they've approached their bio; a useful site for bio searches is ManageFitter (https://www.manageflitter.com/). Though it cannot be stressed enough that having an original and relevant, humorous bio can create an impression that makes the difference between scrolling and clicking follow.

So what to write? Give your bio some personality; it should be about you as a person or a brand, rather than a description of what you do. Below are some further bios for a local cake shop, by their bios alone; which of these accounts would you most likely follow?

Bio 1:

> "Cakeshop in Shoreditch, cakes delivered throughout East London!"

Bio 2:

> "Connoisseurs of cake, purveyors of good vibes. That really good cake shop that you've heard about!"

The creative challenge is to write a bio with personality, whilst also making sure you're using keywords. Twitter, and every other social media platform, works on the basis of keywords too. You can also draw upon Twitter's business tools to use their keyword planner; this will give suggestions of the keywords people are actually using to find people and businesses like yours.

By all means, use an emoji or two to convey a message about you or your brand; however, just like hashtags, it is important to not overdo it. You might also use the bio space to show off your rewards or social proof; try not to brag and be honest if you're displaying reviews. It is also important to have an accurate location added in the location field provided by Twitter. This will allow potential users to locate you.

Chapter 8: What is SEO and Why Does it Matter?

Marc Bonne and Wasim Ahmed

SEO means 'Search Engine Optimization'. If you don't have your own website or are just starting out in business you may have heard of this and know it is something to do with search engines but you might be unsure exactly how it works.

It comes down to how search engines read websites, web pages and pretty much any other content on the internet. Google crawls websites at a rate of millions per second. It then indexes those websites on the basis of keywords. For example, if you have a dog grooming business and your website or Twitter page is full of the keywords 'dog grooming', you would appear in the search results if a user were to search for something like 'dog grooming near me'.

It is almost certain your website will appear in search results, as millions of pages appear when searching with a query. However, the exact page number within search results is a different matter altogether. It's not as simple as just using the words dog grooming over and over again. That won't get you to the first page of results on Google nor Twitter!

Google also crawls Twitter, meaning every tweet, every character that you write on Twitter is indexed and saved by Google and then ranked in results based on the keywords used in those tweets. Where you place in the results will depend on how much authority your account has. Google measures this by how many backlinks a Twitter account has, amongst a myriad of other algorithmic indicators.

If a hyperlink to your Twitter account appears on a number of authority websites or if it is referred to by a blog, which Google deems an authority on a topic, then you will rank higher than others who don't. For instance, if the Guardian newspaper, a series of dog grooming blogs and local directories have a link to your Twitter page, then your Twitter account will have a higher chance of being indexed high up in the ranks.

So you may be wondering where you can find a list of keywords you can use. There are a number of tools online which will help you do this. The first is Google's Keyword Planner (https://ads.google.com/intl/en_uk/home/tools/keyword-planner/). You can use that tool to find out all the relevant keywords in your industry. You can type in dog grooming and it will give you relevant related keywords in a list format that you can use throughout your Twitter posts and your website. It also lets you know how much competition there is for those keywords.

Competition is ranked low, medium or high and indicates how many of your competitors are using the same keywords. There is also lots of data about how much search volume there is for those keywords. That means the number of users every month using any given keyword or combination of those words. Ideally, you will want to use keywords with a low or medium competition level, as well as a high monthly search volume in excess of 10,000 searches.

As part of the Twitter business tools suite, you can also lookup keywords used by Twitter users specifically. It works in much the same way as Google's Keyword Planner does and is intuitive, so anyone can understand it.

You should include keywords in your posts, your bio and other content you create for Twitter. The key is consistency; you need to remember to add keywords to the posts, as well as create engaging content at the same time. Whilst you should be tasteful with the number of keywords used, we recommend that you use at least 1 per post.

The profile picture of your account should either be a clear headshot if it is a personal Twitter profile; businesses should use their logo or a distinctive variation of their logo. People may be more likely to trust faces more that they've seen multiple times, which is why a photo of your face works best.

Some logos are too dark, contain too much text or too squished to be instantly recognizable. Many companies will create a Twitter/social media logo with perhaps the first initial of their main brand name in the same colors and fonts as their original logo.

Your header is by far the largest display space you will ever have on Twitter so it is important you utilize it correctly. The first thing to note is dimensions, you should create a .png file that is 1500px x 500px; this is because whilst Twitter does allow you to upload other dimensions, the image almost is always blurry or doesn't look good on all screen sizes including tablet and mobile.

When you design the header, remember the top part of your profile picture always bleeds onto the header. Therefore you should avoid any texts towards the bottom of the header, as it may be partially hidden on some screen sizes by your profile picture.

There are some simple rules to follow when designing the banner;

1. Don't include your logo in the banner as it takes up valuable space and adds nothing if you're already using it as your profile picture
2. Use high resolution images only, blurry images makes followers run a mile
3. Always use your brand's HEX color codes so you use exactly your brand colors. Never use more than two distinctive brand colors.
4. Keep the most important parts of the header in the center of the banner.

Direct message marketing can be an effective way to speak to customers directly. Everyone will accept how annoying direct messages from companies and even self-promoting individuals can be. Therefore, before you set out on a direct marketing campaign, you should always ask yourself, would I find this annoying?

Direct message marketing works best when you keep what you want to say short and sweet and have a call to action. The main body text should rarely exceed one paragraph; it should be rounded off, asking the user to perform a specific action. That might be as simple as replying to your message, filling in a form or visiting your website.

Direct messaging doesn't need to be time-consuming. By no means will you need to sit there day after day sending out hundreds of messages. There are now tools that can do that for you. One such tool is 'If That Then This', an online service that lets you perform a number of Twitter actions automatically.

Whether it's automatically thanking new Twitter followers, publishing your Instagram photos automatically to Twitter, or sending out direct messages.

Writing a template that will speak to your audience is no easy feat. Why should anyone visit your website, follow you or do anything for that matter? You need an incentive, something of value, to encourage the user to do what you want. Some offer a free eBook, exclusive discount or free gift or services.

You should ask yourself the question, is the incentive I am offering enough to make me bite? Have I been offered something similar and as a result, engaged with that brand?

Chapter 9: Influencers

Wasim Ahmed and Marc Bonne

An influencer is a person or brand that has a large reach and influence over what their followers do. Being an influencer has become a full-time profession for some people who may be earning a lot of money.

Influencers typically have an audience in excess of 100,000 followers and have an affinity and connection with the users they engage with. However, in recent years, 'micro-influencers' have also become established and these types of influencers may have less users following them.

Getting influencers to engage with you in conversation could mean big things for your brand. This is because if an influencer mentions your account, product or service, you're gaining exposure to their audience, an audience who wants to be like the influencer, eat what they eat, do what they do etc.

There are many ways to engage with influencers; you may have the resources to offer the influencer a 'brand deal', which works by contacting their management team (the details of which you will definitely find on their profile) and making an offer on a per post basis. This is essentially a negotiation, so never accept their first price!

For influencers with a smaller following, it may be enough to just send them a sample of your product and offer a per sale affiliate deal. Most major brands including McDonald's, Coca-Cola, Apple and Spotify just to name a few, now have an influencer strategy. It is also possible to pinpoint influencers using tools such as NodeXL (https://www.smrfoundation.org/nodexl/). NodeXL allows you to analyse and visualize any topic on Twitter to identify top hashtags, words, and influential users among many other useful metrics.

Chapter 10: Twitter Analytics

Marc Bonne and Wasim Ahmed

Twitter analytics (https://analytics.twitter.com/) will give you insights into who your users are, their gender, age and so much more. It also gives you a breakdown, tweet by tweet, of how effective your content is. Twitter gives you far more access than other social media platforms when it comes to understanding your followers and their behavior. You should be responsive to what works and what doesn't; the numbers do not lie. Many brands fail to properly utilize the tools that Twitter makes available; they post the same generic content and wonder why they fail to get engagement.

You must go further than just posting content; you must engage in conversation. This is fundamental to how Twitter works. It was invented to facilitate conversations online. Therefore, you should ask questions, give answers, make comments on the world around you and respond to current events in your industry. The more users (particularly those with a lot of followers) 'mention' your account, the more exposure you get. Remember when you are conversing and sharing with another Twitter account, your profile is gaining exposure to their potentially-huge audience.

You can do this using Tweet Deck (https://tweetdeck.twitter.com/). It gives you a complete real-time overview of your presence on Twitter including tweets, private messages, engagements (retweets, likes etc.). The interface comprises of columns, which you can customize to fit your preferences. Looking at your Twitter account in this way makes it easier to manage and helps you to organize your online presence without it all being overwhelming.

There are also many other advanced monitoring, analytics, and analysis tools that have been used by brands to gain insight from Twitter. Table 10.1 below (adapted from Ahmed, 2019) provides an overview of additional analytics tools.

Table 10.1 Overview of Tools for Twitter Analytics

Tool	OS	Download/ Access from
Audience	Web-based	https://audiense.com/
Brand24	Web-based	https://brand24.com/features/#4
Brandwatch	Web-based	https://www.brandwatch.com/
Chorus (free)	Windows (Desktop advisable)	http://chorusanalytics.co.uk/chorus/request_download.php
COSMOS Project (free)	Windows & MAC OS X	http://socialdatalab.net/software
Echosec	Web-based	https://www.echosec.net

Followthehasht ag	Web-based	http://www.followtheh ashtag.com
IBM Bluemix	Web-based	https://www.ibm.com/ cloud-computing/bluemix
Keyhole	Web-based	https://keyhole.co/
Mozdeh (free)	Windows (Desktop advisable)	http://mozdeh.wlv.ac.u k/installation.html
Netlytic	Web-based	https://netlytic.org
NodeXL	Windows	https://www.smrfound ation.org/nodexl/
Nvivo	Windows and MAC	http://www.qsrinternat ional.com/product
Pulsar Social	Web-based	http://www.pulsarplatf orm.com
Social Elephants	Web-based	https://socialelephants. com/en/
Symplur (Healthcare focus)	Web-based	https://www.symplur.c om/
SocioViz	Web-based	http://socioviz.net
Trendsmap	Web-based	https://www.trendsma p.com

Trackmyhashtag	Web-based	https://www.trackmyhashtag.com/
Twitonomy	Web-based	http://www.twitonomy.com
Twitter Arching Google Spreadsheet (TAGS) (free)	Web-based	https://tags.hawksey.info
Visibrain	Web-based	http://www.visibrain.com
Webometric Analyst (free)	Windows	http://lexiurl.wlv.ac.uk

References

Ahmed, W. (2019) Using Twitter as a data source: An overview of current social media research tools (Updated for 2019) *LSE Impact of Social Sciences blog*
[Online] Available at:
https://blogs.lse.ac.uk/impactofsocialsciences/2019/06/18/using-twitter-as-a-data-source-an-overview-of-social-media-research-tools-2019/ [Last Accessed 26/12/2019]

Chapter 11: Making the Most of Twitter

Wasim Ahmed and Marc Bonne

Twitter is an amazing marketing tool, and never before have we had access to such a large audience of people all in the same place at once. Imagine Twitter like a marketplace; you have to compete with other vendors for customer attention, build rapport and persuade to purchase. You still need to pay rent for your spot; however, the currency you use is content and it is due every day.

There are so many free tools out there, many of which we have touched on in the book, but there are so many we haven't. These tools, when used correctly, will help you build a massive following and get noticed in the marketplace.

Putting in the work during the early days will pay dividends in the future; don't give up because you don't have a million followers in the first month. Accept that you're on Twitter (and all social networks) for the long term; be consistent and evolve your Twitter strategy. Be open and transparent with your audience. Your human appeal is what will speak to customers, **not** gimmicky advertising.

Don't be shy either; if something stirs up interest, shock, awe or excitement within, you tweet about it! Marketing is only one side of the coin, Twitter is a free for all and if you fail to deliver what you promise, Twitter will bite back. Ensure your business processes are functioning well and you have a quality product or service, or Twitter could very well be your undoing.

Lastly, enjoy it! If it feels like work, you're not doing it right. Some people are better at creating original content than others and have grown up in a digital age. It might be an idea if you're not getting the engagement or reach you're hoping for; pass your account to another staff member or hire the services of a digital agency. Social media has radically changed the marketing landscape and indeed, all of our lives. With the average person spending many of their waking hours scrolling, you will have to put the work in to stand out.

s

Printed in Great Britain
by Amazon

36062368R10026